A Note From Rick Renner

I am on a personal quest to see a "revival of the Bible" so people can establish their lives on a firm foundation that will stand strong and endure the test as the end-time storm winds begin to intensify.

In order to experience a revival of the Bible in your personal life, it is important to take time each day to read, receive, and apply its truths to your life. James tells us that if we will continue in the perfect law of liberty — refusing to be forgetful hearers but determined to be doers — we will be blessed in our ways. As you watch or listen to the programs in this series and work through this corresponding study guide, I trust that you will search the Scriptures and allow the Holy Spirit to help you hear something new from God's Word that applies specifically to your life. I encourage you to be a doer of the Word that He reveals to you. Whatever the cost, I assure you — it will be worth it.

> Thy words were found, and I did eat them;
> and thy word was unto me the joy and rejoicing of mine heart:
> for I am called by thy name, O Lord God of hosts.
> — Jeremiah 15:16

Your brother and friend in Jesus Christ,

Rick Renner

Resting in Our Redemption

Copyright © 2021 by Rick Renner
8316 E. 73rd St.
Tulsa, Oklahoma 74133

Published by Rick Renner Ministries
www.renner.org

ISBN 13: 978-1-68031-829-6

eBook ISBN 13: 978-1-68031-830-2

How To Use This Study Guide

This five-lesson study guide corresponds to *"Resting in Our Redemption"* *With Rick Renner* (Renner TV). Each lesson in this study guide covers a topic that is addressed during the program series, with questions and references supplied to draw you deeper into your own private study of the Scriptures on this subject.

To derive the most benefit from this study guide, consider the following:

First, watch or listen to the program prior to working through the corresponding lesson in this guide. (Programs can also be viewed at **renner.org** by clicking on the Media/Archives links.)

Second, take the time to look up the scriptures included in each lesson. Prayerfully consider their application to your own life.

Third, use a journal or notebook to make note of your answers to each lesson's Study Questions and Practical Application challenges.

Fourth, invest specific time in prayer and in the Word of God to consult with the Holy Spirit. Write down the scriptures or insights He reveals to you.

Finally, take action! Whatever the Lord tells you to do according to His Word, do it.

For added insights on this subject, it is recommended that you obtain Rick Renner's book *Dressed To Kill: A Biblical Approach to Spiritual Warfare and Armor.* You may also select from Rick's other available resources by placing your order at **renner.org** or by calling 1-800-742-5593.

TOPIC

Why Does the Battle Still Rage?

SCRIPTURES

1. **Psalm 107:2** — Let the redeemed of the Lord say so, whom he hath redeemed from the hand of the enemy.

2. **Colossians 1:13** — Who hath delivered us from the power of darkness, and hath translated us into the kingdom of his dear Son.

3. **Romans 12:2** — And be not conformed to this world: but be ye transformed by the renewing of your mind....

4. **Ephesians 4:23** — And be renewed in the spirit of your mind.

5. **Colossians 3:10** — And have put on the new man, which is renewed in knowledge after the image of him that created him.

6. **1 Peter 1:13** — Wherefore gird up the loins of your mind....

GREEK WORDS

1. "delivered" — **ῥύομαι** (*rhuomai*): to rescue; to snatch from danger; to deliver; removing someone from danger or oppression; snatched just in the nick of time

2. "from" — **ἐκ** (*ek*): out; from

3. "power" — **ἐξουσία** (*exousia*): authority; control; dominion; influence; power

4. "darkness" — **σκότος** (*skotos*): darkness and everything connected with darkness

5. "translated" — **μεθίστημι** (*methistimi*): to transfer from one place to another place

6. "gird up" — **ἀναζώννυμι** (*anadzonnumi*): pictures runners who would gather up their loose robes and tuck them up under their girdle before they started to run; to run with no distractions; to remove the encumbrance of dangling, loosely hanging clothes that would hinder one's steps or plans; pictures putting away loose ends

SYNOPSIS

The five lessons in this study on *Resting in Our Redemption* will focus on the following topics:

- Why Does the Battle Still Rage?
- Satan's Slave Market
- Purchased Out of Slavery
- Paying the Demanded Price
- Restored to Full Status

The emphasis of this lesson:

Through faith in the completed work of Jesus Christ, we are redeemed — we are totally set free from Satan's power and dominion and no longer slaves to sin. To experience and fully enjoy the benefits of our redemption, we must continually renew our minds with the truth of God's Word. Otherwise, we will live in the illusion of bondage.

What Does It Mean To Be *Redeemed*?

Have you ever stopped to think about your redemption? Most of us have sung songs about being redeemed by Jesus, but we don't really understand what He did. The fact is, when God created the heavens and the earth and the first people — Adam and Eve — everything was perfect. But when Adam and Eve chose to disobey God, sin and death entered the world, and all of mankind came under the dominion of Satan. You might say we were swallowed up into Satan's will and enslaved to do his bidding. Since no human being could be good enough or work hard enough to get back into right relationship with God, God came to humanity in the form of Jesus Christ. Jesus lived a sinless life and died a criminal's death to pay the price for our sins. Through faith in Him, we are *redeemed!*

There are four different Greek words used in the New Testament to denote "redemption." These include: *agoradzo, exagoradzo, lutroo,* and *apolutrosis.* All four of these terms are derived from the concept of the slave market in the First Century. When a buyer entered the slave market and saw a slave that he wanted, he would pay the price demanded for him. In a similar way, when Jesus came to earth, He entered into the slave market of humanity and saw us in slavery to sin. He took one look at us and made the decision right then and there to purchase us — to redeem us — and make us His own. And the price He paid was the highest price ever paid for a slave: He paid with His own blood.

In Psalm 107:2, the psalmist said, "Let the redeemed of the Lord say so, whom he hath redeemed from the hand of the enemy." If you have repented of your sins and invited Jesus to be the Lord and Savior of your life, you are redeemed! God has delivered you from Satan's slave market and adopted you into His family to forever be with Him! He has set you free from the power of darkness and translated you into the kingdom of Jesus, His dear Son (*see* Colossians 1:13).

Jesus Came to Earth on a Rescue Mission

The apostle Paul talks about our liberation from Satan in his letter to the believers in Colossae. He said, "[God] Who hath delivered us from the power of darkness, and hath translated us into the kingdom of his dear Son: in whom we have redemption through his blood, even forgiveness of sins" (Colossians 1:13,14).

There are several important words in this passage, including the word "delivered." In Greek, this is the word *rhuomai*, which means *to rescue*; *to snatch from danger*, or *to deliver*. It depicts *removing someone from danger or oppression* and carries the idea of being *snatched just in the nick of time*. The use of this word tells us that when Jesus came, He was on a divine *rescue mission*. He came to snatch us out of the enemy's dominion, and He did it just in the nick of time!

Also notice the word "from." Paul said God "…delivered us *from* the power of darkness…" (Colossians 1:13). This word "from" is the Greek word *ek*, which means *from* or *right out of.* Jesus snatched us *right out of* the "power of darkness." The word "power" here is the Greek word *exousia*, and it denotes *authority; control; dominion; influence* or *power*. And the word "darkness" in Greek is the word *skotos*, which describes *darkness* and *everything connected with darkness*.

The moment we repented of our sins and asked Jesus into our life, the Bible says God "…translated us into the kingdom of his dear Son" (Colossians 1:13). The word "translated" in Greek is *methistimi*, and it means *to transfer from one place to another place.* When you got saved, you were transferred out of the kingdom of darkness into the kingdom of light

— you were rescued from Satan's slave market and adopted into God's family. This is a vivid picture of redemption.

Are You Living in the Illusion of Bondage?

Romans 6:23 says, "For the wages of sin is death; but the gift of God is eternal life through Jesus Christ our Lord." Jesus paid the wages for our sin through His death. His life's blood canceled all the devil's rights to us and completely freed us from his control. This is what it means to be *redeemed*. And through our redemption, we have Christ's healing and His total deliverance.

You may be thinking, *If I'm redeemed and set free from Satan's authority, control, and dominion, why does it seem like the battle is still raging in my life? And if healing and deliverance are a part of our redemption, why am I still dealing with sickness and trying to break free from bad habits?* Good questions. And one of the best ways to answer them is with this true story Rick shared in his book *Dressed To Kill*:

> "Several years ago, the police called a friend of mine in the middle of the night, informing him that one of his animals, a goat, had gotten out of his property and had been hit and killed by a car. My friend quickly put on his jacket and rushed to the place where the dead goat was supposed to be lying.
>
> However, when he arrived at the scene, he discovered that the goat wasn't dead at all. Someone had stolen the goat, tied up its legs with rope so it couldn't move, and then dumped the goat along the side of the road.
>
> My friend reached over, untied the rope that held the goat captive, and then slapped it and said, 'Get up!' But the goat just lay there as though it was still bound and unable to move. Once again, he slapped the goat and said, 'Get up!' But the goat continued to lie on its side as if it were incapable of moving.
>
> The man began examining the goat, looking for a wound that was possibly keeping it from getting up. Then he noticed that the animal's legs were still tightly clinging to each other as though they were still tied with ropes. The problem then became clear: the goat thought it was still bound!

So my friend bent over and picked up the goat, set it on its feet, and slapped it again, telling it to 'Get up!' Finally, the goat realized its feet were no longer bound and began to jump and leap in its newfound freedom."[1]

The truth is, many Christians are just like the goat in this story. All of us were previously held captive by Satan's destructive power. He had tied us up in his slavery and then dumped us off in a dark, secluded place waiting for destruction to completely run its course.

Then we heard and received the Gospel message and were born again. The Spirit of Christ came to live inside of us and "untie" Satan's bonds from our lives. Through Jesus' redemptive work on the Cross, He legally removed the bondages that had us bound. However, even though this liberating work has been done, if we're not aware of it, *we remain bound because we are living in the illusion of bondage.*

Just like the goat owner looked at his goat and said, "Get up!" Jesus is looking at us and saying, "Get up! And get moving! I've already untied all the bondages from your life. I've paid the price for your freedom with my own blood. Stop living in the illusion of bondage. You are redeemed!"

Break Free From the Illusion by Renewing Your Mind

As a believer, one of the most important habits you must develop and put into practice is *renewing your mind.* The freedom Christ bought for you becomes a way of life only as you replace wrong thinking and wrong believing with what the Word of God declares about your new condition in Christ. Although your inner man has been born again and made completely new (*see* Second Corinthians 5:17), your mind and body must be conformed to the image of Christ. This is what the Bible calls *sanctification* — it is the process of "working out your salvation" through the power of the Holy Spirit (*see* Philippians 2:12,13).

Wrong thinking, wrong believing, and memories of terrible experiences will only serve to keep you living in the illusion of bondage. As you really begin to dig into the Word of God, His truth exposes the lies you are believing and the fears that are paralyzing you from moving forward. Day by day as you soak in the Scriptures, wrong mindsets transferred to you through your parents, family members, teachers, and friends are uncovered and gradually replaced with truth.

Make no mistake: Satan knows very well the importance of the mind. It is the strategic control center of our life. If he can take control of one small area in your thinking, he can begin to expand his influence into other weak areas of your mind that have not been renewed and strengthened by the Word of God and the power of the Holy Spirit. For this reason, God has commanded us again and again to renew our minds. He said:

- **"...Be ye transformed by the renewing of your mind, that ye may prove what is that good, and acceptable, and perfect, will of God"** (**Romans 12:2**).

- **"...Be renewed in the spirit of your mind; and ... put on the new man, which after God is created in righteousness and true holiness"** (**Ephesians 4:23,24**).

- **"...Put on the new man, which is renewed in knowledge after the image of him that created him"** (**Colossians 3:10**).

- **"Let the word of Christ dwell in you richly in all wisdom..."** (**Colossians 3:16**).

The truth is, renewing your mind with God's Word regularly is the foundation of spiritual warfare. The very first weapon in the armor of God is the belt of truth, which is the written Word of God. It is the only visible, tangible piece of weaponry, and all the other pieces of armor are connected to it. Only with the Word of truth regularly renewing your mind can you be clothed in righteousness and peace, have knowledge of your salvation, take up the shield of faith, wield the sword of the Spirit, and pray with all kinds of prayers. Renewing your mind with the Word is a lifelong commitment that produces far-reaching benefits.

'Gird Up the Loins of Your Mind'

Like the apostle Paul, Peter also emphasized the importance of renewing our minds. He said, "Wherefore gird up the loins of your mind..." (1 Peter 1:13). Notice the strange phrase "gird up." It is a translation of the Greek word *anadzonnumi*, which pictures runners who would gather up their loose robes and tuck them up under their girdle (or belt) before they started to run. Essentially, this word means *to run with no distractions; to remove the encumbrance of dangling, loosely hanging clothes that would hinder one's steps or plans.* It is the picture of one putting away loose ends.

To "gird up" the loins of your mind, you must renew your thinking with God's Word. The continual renewal of your mind with the truth of Scripture will eradicate wrong thinking, wrong believing, scars from the past, and hurtful, emotional memories that would exert their influence over your new life in Christ. Otherwise, those loose, dangling, unsurrendered, and unrenewed areas of your mind will be used by the devil to trip you up and bring you crashing to the ground. To "gird up the loins of your mind" means to feed your soul and spirit the Word of God, allowing it to grab hold of all the loose, dangling hindrances in your thinking and your emotions and get them out of your way so you can successfully run the race God has set before you.

To be clear — you cannot just *ignore* wrong thinking and wrong believing and expect it to just go away. Ignoring incorrect thinking and believing will only allow it to continue dominating your life and impairing your ability to get up, get moving, and enjoy the full benefits of your redemption in Christ.

Friend, you have been redeemed by the Blood of the Lamb! Jesus loves you so much that He gave His very life so you would be delivered out of the power of darkness and translated into the kingdom of light. Satan's control and dominion over you have been totally destroyed. If you're not experiencing the full benefits of your redemption, begin to dig into God's Word daily and ask the Holy Spirit to renew your mind.

STUDY QUESTIONS

Study to shew thyself approved unto God, a workman that needeth not to be ashamed, rightly dividing the word of truth.
— 2 Timothy 2:15

1. Through Peter, God instructs you to "gird up the loins of your mind," which means to feed your soul and spirit the Word of God, and allow it to grab hold of all the loose, dangling hindrances in your thinking and your emotions. Are you obeying this command from God? Do you have loose, dangling, unrenewed and unsurrendered areas of your mind?

2. Those places in your mind that are not surrendered to God and unrenewed with His Word are places where Satan seeks to establish his *strongholds*. A *stronghold* is an area or wrong thinking that has a **strong** *hold* on you. In other words, it is an area where you effortlessly gravitate toward doing wrong — it's like second nature, and you can't seem to break free. Where do you think you have strongholds?

3. Common strongholds people deal with include things like worry, fear, condemnation, and anger. Taking your answers from question 2, use a Bible concordance to identify verses that combat these areas of wrong thinking. Then begin to *read through* and *meditate* on these passages daily to renew your mind. A few examples are provided.

- **WORRY**: Matthew 6:25-34 _____

  _____

- **FEAR**: 2 Timothy 1:7 _____

  _____

- **CONDEMNATION**: Romans 8:1 _____

  _____

- **ANGER**: Ephesians 4:26,27 _____

  _____

PRACTICAL APPLICATION

But be ye doers of the word, and not hearers only,
deceiving your own selves.
— James 1:22

1. Prior to this lesson, what did you understand about your redemption in Christ? What truths from the Word of God is He making real to you in this teaching?

2. The Bible declares that God "…hath delivered us from the power of darkness, and hath translated us into the kingdom of his dear Son" (Colossians 1:13). The question is, are you living in the *illusion of bondage*? In what ways are you like that goat that had been untied and set free but still lying on the ground thinking it was captive?

3. As a believer, one of the most important habits you must develop and put into practice is *renewing your mind*. Be honest: When was the last time you sat still and really soaked in the Scriptures? What can you *decrease* in your daily routine in order to *increase* time in God's Word?

As you cultivate this healthy practice, consider getting a good translation of the Bible you understand and a notebook where you can write scriptures and topically arrange them to frequently refer back to.

---

[1] Rick Renner, *Dressed To Kill* (Tulsa, OK: Harrison House, 1991, paperback edition 2015), pp. 103-104.

LESSON 2

TOPIC

Satan's Slave Market

SCRIPTURES

1. **Psalm 107:2** — Let the redeemed of the Lord say so, whom he hath redeemed from the hand of the enemy.

2. **Ephesians 1:7** — In whom we have redemption through his blood, the forgiveness of sins, according to the riches of his grace.

3. **1 Corinthians 6:20** — For ye are bought with a price....

4. **Romans 7:14** — For we know that the law is spiritual: but I am carnal, sold under sin.

5. **Romans 6:17,20** — But God be thanked, that ye were the servants of sin, but ye have obeyed from the heart that form of doctrine which was delivered you. For when ye were the servants of sin, ye were free from righteousness.

6. **Colossians 1:21** — And you, that were sometime alienated and enemies in your mind by wicked works, yet now hath he reconciled.

GREEK WORDS

1. "bought" — ἀγοράζω (*agoradzo*): to purchase in the marketplace; often used to denote the purchase of a slave out of the slave market; to transfer ownership from a seller to a buyer; to redeem

2. "sold" — πιπράσκω (*piprasko*): like a product for purchase, it pictures a slave being transferred into the ownership of a new master

3. "servant" — δοῦλος (*doulos*): the most abject term for a slave in the New Testament; one totally sold into slavery; a perpetual slave for life; one bound to do the bidding of his owner; a slave whose principal task was to fulfill the desires of his master for the rest of his life; this servant's existence was to service his master in whatever way the master asked or demanded; pictures one whose will is completely swallowed up in the will of another

SYNOPSIS

During the First Century, the ancient city of Ephesus was home to one of the largest slave markets in the entire Roman Empire. People came from all across the region to buy and sell slaves. Human beings, created in the image of God, were trafficked, and treated like trash; a very nauseating and disgusting sight to see that should never have been permitted.

The apostle Paul developed the concept of our redemption in Christ from the idea of the slave market — specifically the slave market he had seen in the city of Ephesus. In order to truly understand what it means to be redeemed, you have to understand how it relates to the slave market.

In Greek, the word for market is *agora*, and Paul used this word to explain what Jesus did for us through the Cross. When Jesus came into the world, every human being was a spiritual slave in Satan's slave market. With His own Blood, Jesus paid the price to purchase us out of that slave market and set us free from Satan's dominion and the power of sin.

The emphasis of this lesson:

The moment Adam and Eve disobeyed God in the Garden of Eden, all of mankind was transferred from God's hands into the hands of a new owner — Satan. We were taken captive into Satan's slave market and became "servants of sin," swallowed up in Satan's will. Jesus' sole purpose in coming to earth was to purchase us out of this marketplace and set us free from Satan's dominion and the power of sin.

Our freedom from Satan's power was extremely expensive. In fact, it was the highest price ever paid in human history to redeem a slave. The price Jesus paid to set us free from the devil's ownership was His own blood. Ephesians 1:7 says, "In whom we have redemption *through his blood*, the forgiveness of sins, according to the riches of his grace."

Then in First Corinthians 6:20, Paul adds to this by saying, "For ye are bought with a price...."The word "bought" here is very important. It is the Greek word *agoradzo*, which is taken from the root word *agora* — the term for *marketplace*. *Agoradzo* means *to purchase in the marketplace*, and it can also be translated *to redeem*. It signifies *the transfer of ownership from a seller to a buyer*, and it was often used to denote *the purchase of a slave out of the slave market*.

The Slave Market of the Roman World

One of the most dreadful and deplorable places on the face of the earth was the ancient Roman slave market. Taken from adaptations of his book, *A Light in Darkness*, Rick paints a vivid picture of this loathsome place:

> "First Century Ephesus had a growing population. A large part of the growing population was the slave community. There were two different categories of slaves in the Roman world: public slaves and private slaves. Public slaves were owned by the state and were used in great numbers to assist in the massive building projects that were being constructed all over the Roman Empire. But private slaves were owned by private individuals, or by private families, and generally possessed less freedom then public slaves.
>
> Slavery was such a central part of Roman society that slaves could be found in almost every sphere of life. Roman slaves were either born into slavery or became slaves due to a variety of circumstances. Military conquests brought a constant stream of new slaves to stand on the auction blocks of Roman slave markets. And such was the case for the slave market in Ephesus — one of the largest in the entire Roman Empire during the First Century.
>
> Roman slave markets were disgusting and deplorable places where human beings were paraded in front of potential buyers and then put on auction blocks to be sold to the highest bidder. But before this buying, selling, and trading of human beings commenced, the buyers were permitted to 'inspect the merchandise.'
>
> For instance, a slave's value was largely determined by the condition of his teeth. If he had good teeth, he was probably in decent physical condition and therefore more expensive. If his teeth were rotten, he could be purchased for a lesser price. Therefore, a potential buyer would usually shove back a slave's head, force

open his mouth, and inspect his teeth to see if they were decayed or in fairly good shape.

If a slave was going to be used in menial work requiring a great deal of physical abuse, then potential buyers were allowed to spit in the slaves' faces, slap them, and even curse at them to see how much abuse the slave could endure. If a slave could swallow his pride, grit his teeth, and hold his temper during this humiliating abuse, it was assumed he could be used for hard manual labor without giving his new owner a lot of trouble.

Once a slave had been purchased, he was considered the legal property of his master. And in the Roman world a slave owner could do anything he wished with his slaves. He could abuse them, molest them, or even kill them if he wished to do so. Since slaves were considered a master's property, the master could also sell them, lend them out to friends, or even rent them to other people who needed a slave. And slaves in the Roman Empire were often whipped and treated with cruelty."[2]

It has been suggested that the slave population in Asia, which is where Ephesus was located, was greater in number than in any other part of the Roman Empire. During the First Century when the Church was birthed, historians estimate that Ephesus had a population of 250,000 people, and of that number, it is believed there were approximately 60,000 slaves.

Clearly, slavery was a very central part of life — not only in Ephesus, but also in Rome, Corinth, and all across the Roman Empire. There were even many people in the Church that were slaves. And because it was such a dominant fixture in society, people were forced to deal with it on a regular basis.

Before We Came to Christ, We Were Swallowed Up in Satan's Will

Through Adam's disobedience, spiritual death seized humanity. The Bible says, "...By one man sin entered into the world, and death by sin; and so death passed upon all men, for that all have sinned" (Romans 5:12). With each generation after Adam, spiritual death drove people of all nations, tribes, and ethnic groups deeper and deeper into slavery to sin and world-wide depravity.

Our bondage at that time was so complete that the apostle Paul said we were "...sold under sin" (Romans 7:14). That word "sold" is taken from the Greek word *piprasko*, which is also a word borrowed from the slave market. It describes *a product for purchase* and literally depicts *a transfer of property*. In this particular verse it pictures *a slave being transferred into the ownership of a new master*. By using this word, Paul is telling us that mankind had been transferred from God's hands into the hands of a new owner — Satan. And before Jesus came into our lives, Satan had total ownership of us.

Like slaves in a slave market, we stood on the auction block helpless as Satan slapped our lives around — hitting us, kicking us, spitting in our faces, and abusing us in any way he desired. Our "slave owner" worked tirelessly to destroy our self-image, devastate our bodies with all types of sin and vices, and mar us emotionally. When he finished using one kind of bondage and death on us, he would put us back on the trading block to be auctioned off again, allowing yet another form of bondage to enslave us and begin to leave its destructive marks on our lives.

Thus, we were passed from one bondage to the next in a never-ending cycle of devastation and defeat. With each passing day, whether we were aware of it or not, we were being sold deeper and deeper into the captivity of sin — lock, stock, and barrel, from the inside out, every inch from head to toe. This is why Paul described us as "the servants of sin" in Romans 6:17 and 20.

The word "servant" is derived from the Greek word *doulos*, which is the most abject term for a slave in the New Testament. It depicts *one totally sold into slavery; a perpetual slave for life*. It denotes *one bound to do the bidding of his owner; a slave whose principal task was to fulfill the desires of his master for the rest of his life*. This servant's existence was to service his master in whatever way the master asked or demanded. It is a picture of one whose will is completely swallowed up in the will of another.

Don't miss this: The use of this word *doulos* — translated here as "servant" — means that before we were saved, we were "swallowed up" in the will of Satan. Although we may have thought that we were in charge of our lives and calling the shots, in reality, we were abject slaves to sin, and our destinies were being orchestrated by an unseen, diabolical spirit that wanted to destroy us.

Our pre-salvation slavery to the devil was so entrenched that our nature became filled with rebellion, and the chasm between God and us became so great that the Bible says we became "alienated and enemies" in our minds through wicked works (*see* Colossians 1:21).

Then Jesus Came and 'Bought' Us With His Blood

When Jesus entered the world nearly 2,000 years ago, the world itself had become a disgusting, nauseating spiritual slave market — an *agoradzo*. All mankind was completely lost and taken captive by Satan, who had a death-grip on the hearts of men and women and had filled their natures with violence and destruction. It was into this death-permeated, demonically energized world that Jesus — the Creator of the heavens and the earth — was birthed.

God sent His own Son right into the very middle of Satan's slave market with one purpose: to pay the price that was required to secure man's deliverance from bondage to Satan once and for all. We have been "bought with a price," and that price was the precious blood of Jesus! Again, that word "bought" is the Greek word *agoradzo*, which depicts Jesus purchasing us out of Satan's slave market. We are no longer under the devil's dominion. *The transfer of our ownership has moved from Satan to Jesus!*

As a born-again child of God, you are no longer your own (*see* 1 Corinthians 6:19). You belong to Jesus — body, soul, and spirit. In fact, your body is the temple of His Holy Spirit. This is why Paul said, "…Glorify God in your body, and in your spirit, which are God's" (1 Corinthians 6:20). It is God's desire that you live in all of His goodness. We are His children who have been translated out of the kingdom of darkness and into the kingdom of His dear Son — a kingdom where there is no worry, no fear, no sickness, no poverty, and no brokenness. Praise His Name!

In our next lesson, we will explore the second Greek word for "redemption" — the word *exagoradzo*. It focuses on Jesus' ultimate intention, which was to not just buy us out of slavery, but to set us free from slavery permanently.

STUDY QUESTIONS

**Study to shew thyself approved unto God, a workman that needeth
not to be ashamed, rightly dividing the word of truth.**
— 2 Timothy 2:15

1. What new insights did you learn about the slave market in the ancient Roman world? Did you realize that slavery was as extensive as it was during the First Century?

2. The Bible says, "...By one man sin entered into the world, and death by sin; and so death passed upon all men, for that all have sinned" (Romans 5:12). This is a direct reference to Adam's act of disobedience in Eden. What exciting news does God give us about Jesus — in Romans 5:15-19 that counteracts the miserable mess Adam and Eve led us into? (Also consider First Corinthians 15:21,22.)

PRACTICAL APPLICATION

**But be ye doers of the word, and not hearers only,
deceiving your own selves.**
— James 1:22

1. What is your reaction when you hear how human beings were treated — that they were turned into slaves, placed on an auction block, and "inspected as merchandise"?

2. What spiritual parallels can you see between the treatment of slaves in the ancient slave market and the way Satan treats those he has blinded to the Gospel and bound under his control?

3. Every believer has a story of redemption. What is yours? If you had sixty seconds to sum up and shout to the world how Jesus redeemed your life, what would you say? (Think about how the enemy passed you from one bondage to the next in a never-ending cycle of devastation and defeat and briefly share your gratefulness for Jesus' divine rescue.)

---

[2] Rick Renner, *A Light in Darkness* (Tulsa, OK: Harrison House, 2010, 2018), pp. 153-158.

TOPIC

Purchased Out of Slavery

SCRIPTURES

1. **Psalm 107:2** — Let the redeemed of the Lord say so, whom he hath redeemed from the hand of the enemy.

2. **Galatians 3:13** — Christ hath redeemed us from the curse of the law, being made a curse for us....

GREEK WORDS

1. "redeemed" — ἐξαγοράζω (*exagoradzo*): a compound of the words ἐκ (*ek*) and ἀγοράζω (*agoradzo*); ἐκ (*ek*) means out and ἀγοράζω (*agoradzo*) means to purchase in the marketplace; used to denote the purchase of a slave out of the slave market; to transfer ownership from a seller to a buyer; when compounded into ἐξαγοράζω (*exagoradzo*), it pictures one who has come to purchase a slave OUT OF the slave market

SYNOPSIS

The ancient city of Miletus was located in the Roman province of Asia, and it was an amazing city. It sat on the western coast just a few miles due south of the city of Ephesus and featured a magnificent harbor that accommodated the coming and going of people from all across the region. Miletus was a magnet for shoppers. It had several *agoras*, which is the Greek word for *markets*, and as we saw previously, slaves were frequently bought and sold in the marketplace.

When the apostle Paul wrote about Jesus' redemption in our lives, he used the word *agora* and the imagery of the slave market to explain the miraculous liberation we have been given. In our last lesson, we examined the Greek word *agoradzo*, which describes *the process of buying a slave out of the marketplace*, the same word used to describe our *redemption*. The second word for "redemption" we're going to explore is the Greek word *exagoradzo*, which carries the idea of *buying a slave out of the marketplace with the purpose of setting him free forever.*

The emphasis of this lesson:

When Jesus took our punishment and purchased us from Satan's slave market, He not only bought us out of bondage, He also set us free and permanently liberated us from Satan's slavery forever. Unlike most slaves who were bought and then sold again and again, Jesus redeemed us once and for all, never to be sold again.

A Review of Lesson 2

Before our salvation experience, we were all slaves in Satan's slave market lost in a life of sin. Spiritually speaking, he slapped us around — kicking us, beating us, and abusing us in whatever ways he desired.

But then Jesus came into the slave market and saw all of humanity bound by Satan — including you. Moved with extraordinary compassion, He chose to pay the price for our redemption, and that price was His very life. Through the shedding of His blood, Jesus bought us out of Satan's slave market (*agoradzo*) and out of Satan's ownership. Christ is our new owner, and He wants us to glorify Him with our whole life. That is why the Bible says, "For ye are bought (*agoradzo*) with a price: therefore glorify God in your body, and in your spirit, which are God's" (1 Corinthians 6:20).

Friend, if you are redeemed, you need to declare it. Psalm 107:2 says, "Let the redeemed of the Lord say so, whom he hath redeemed from the hand of the enemy." You are no longer under Satan's control, dominion, or power — and no longer a "servant of sin," swallowed up in Satan's will. You are made free by Jesus Christ, and that is great reason to rejoice!

What Were We Really Like Before We Were Saved?

It's important to note that our lives were a complete mess before the grace of God and the blood of Jesus touched us. Remember, Paul said we were "...sold under sin" (Romans 7:14), which means mankind had been transferred from God's hands into the hands of a new owner — Satan. Paul went on to say in his letter to the Ephesians that we, "...were dead in trespasses and sins" (Ephesians 2:1). The word "dead" here is the Greek word *nekros*, and it describes *a lifeless corpse* or *a cadaver with no life left in it*. Spiritually speaking, before salvation, we were like a lifeless corpse. We were not thinking about or looking for God. As dead people, we simply did not have the ability to find God on our own. It was God that was in pursuit of us.

The Bible goes on to say, "Wherein in time past ye walked according to the course of this world, according to the prince of the power of the air, the spirit that now worketh in the children of disobedience" (Ephesians 2:2). The words "according to" are a translation of the Greek word *kata*, which describes *a downward force; domination* or *subjugation*. It can also mean *controlled*. Thus, before we were saved, our lives were *dominated, controlled,* and even *manipulated* by "the course of this world," a phrase which refers to the *organized system of society*.

So who or what is controlling and manipulating "the course of this world"? Paul reveals it in Ephesians 2:2. He said those without Christ live "…according to the prince of the power of the air, the spirit that now worketh in the children of disobedience" (Ephesians 2:2). Again, we see the phrase "according to," which is a translation of the Greek word *kata*, indicating *a downward force that is dominating, subjugating,* and *manipulating*.

The controlling force that is manipulating and dominating the unsaved people in society is "the prince of the power of the air." This is Satan. Although he does not have authority over the universe or over nature, he does have authority in the realm of the world's system, working through people and the whims of the times. He uses things like governments, entertainment, education, fashionable trends, and the court system to achieve his agenda.

As the prince of the power of the air, the Bible says Satan "…now worketh in the children of disobedience" (Ephesians 2:2). The word "worketh" here is the Greek word *energountos*, which is from the word *energeo*, and it describes *energy — a power that energizes or activates*. This word depicts *a powerful force that is set into motion; active power*. In this verse, it signifies *an energizing presence*. Hence, Satan is the *energizing presence* working in the children of disobedience, which included us before we came to Christ.

Before we were saved, our entire life was dominated by the enemy who was working through the fleeting whims of society. We were dead in our sins and had no idea of eternal things. As slaves in Satan's slave market, we were slapped around and brutally abused, being sold from one form of bondage into another. Having control over our mind and emotions, the devil did everything he could to take us down and destroy us. "Energized" by demonic spirits, we were "servants of sin," swallowed up in Satan's will and dominated by sin's power. This was our deplorable condition before Jesus came and "redeemed" us from Satan's slave market.

Jesus' Redemption Permanently Set Us Free

The second Greek word for "redemption" is the word *exagoradzo*. It, too, is derived from the word *agora*, the word for *marketplace*. We find this word in Galatians 3:13, which says, "Christ hath redeemed us from the curse of the law, being made a curse for us...." The word "redeemed" in this passage is the word *exagoradzo*. It is a compound of the words *ek* and *agoradzo*. The word *ek* means *out*, and *agoradzo* means *to purchase in the marketplace*. It denotes the purchase of a slave out of the slave market; to transfer ownership from a seller to a buyer. When these two words are compounded into *exagoradzo*, it pictures *one who has come to purchase a slave OUT OF the slave market forever.*

Rick covers the meaning of this word in greater detail in his book *Dressed To Kill*:

> "*Exagoradzo* conveys the idea of *removal*. Therefore, it signifies *the purchase of a slave in order to permanently set that slave FREE from that heinous place, never to be put on the trading block off slavery again.* The word *exagoradzo* pictures a slave who has been liberated *out of* that stinking, nauseating, disgusting, depraved, and cursed slave market forever!
>
> This word *exagoradzo* is used several times in Paul's epistles to paint a picture of Jesus' redemptive work *to remove us* from slavery. A perfect New Testament example of this word is found in Galatians 3:13, where Paul says, 'Christ hath *redeemed* us from the curse of the law....'"

By using the word *exagoradzo* in connection with Jesus *redeeming* us from the curse of the Law, Paul is telling us plainly that Jesus' sacrificial death not only paid the penalty for our sin, but His death also *removed us* [permanently] from living under the curse forevermore!

…This is what we must understand about God's plan of redemption: His purpose in sending His Son was not just to inspect our condition of slavery and to locate us in our depravity. His ultimate plan, which He accomplished in Jesus Christ's death and resurrection, was to *buy us out of* that miserable condition and to make us His own sons and daughters — forever removed from under the curse of sin and the Law.

However, slaves did not come cheaply. If the auctioneer knew that a buyer really wanted a particular slave, he could demand unbelievably high prices. We must therefore ask, 'What price did Jesus pay for our freedom from Satan's power?'"[3]

Think about that. What price was required to purchase us and to permanently set us free? The Bible says, "But [you were purchased] with the precious blood of Christ (the Messiah), like that of a [sacrificial] lamb without blemish or spot" (1 Peter 1:19 *AMPC*). Indeed, Jesus paid a very high price for our permanent freedom.

Jesus Paid the Highest Price To Set a Slave Free

To give you an even greater understanding of the deep meaning of our "redemption," let's look at the historical background of what it meant to be a slave in biblical times. For this, we turn to Rick's book *Sparkling Gems From the Greek, Volume 1*:

"In New Testament times, slaves could be very *costly*. When a slave purchaser came to the slave market to look for a new slave, he would meander through the aisles of the marketplace, his eyes roaming over all the slaves for sale as he searched for the one he wanted. After pinpointing the slave who seemed to fit his needs, the purchaser was then allowed to inspect the slave's condition. The purpose of this inspection was similar to that of a test drive when a person is checking out a car before he purchases it. Just as every buyer wants to be sure he's getting a good product, every slave buyer wanted to check out the merchandise before he put his money on the table.

The inspection included physically beating the slave to see how he responded to abuse, so the purchaser would know how much 'wear and tear' the slave could take on the job. The buyer was also allowed to pull open the slave's mouth and look at his teeth to see if they were rotten or in good shape as he tried to establish the slave's physical health before making an offer to purchase him.

If the buyer decided to proceed with the purchase after the inspection was complete, it was then time for the next stage of the process — that moment when the slave was put on the auction block. When the auctioneer knew that a buyer really had his eye on a specific slave, he would take that as a signal to push the price for that slave as high as possible. And if the buyer continued to show interest in the same slave, that would let the auctioneer know he could demand a completely unreasonable price and probably get it!

All of these images are contained in the word "redemption."

…At times, a caring and compassionate individual would come to the slave market for the sole purpose of purchasing slaves *out of* slavery to liberate and set them free! In this case, the payment offered was viewed as a *ransom* — paid to obtain freedom for slaves."[4]

When we take into account all this meaning and apply it to the context of our redemption in Christ, it tells us several specific things:

1. Jesus came into the world, which was Satan's slave market, because He was looking for us.
2. Jesus knew He wanted us, and He wouldn't be satisfied until the purchase was complete.
3. Jesus wanted us so much He was willing to pay *any* price demanded to buy us from the slave market.
4. Jesus purchased us with His own blood so we would become His own personal property.
5. Jesus purchased us with His blood — the highest price ever paid for a slave — and gave us a liberating freedom that can only be known because of His work in our lives.

This tells us that our freedom from Satan's ownership was *extremely expensive*. When Jesus came on His rescue mission to set us free, He paid the highest price ever paid to free a slave from bondage. The ransom He paid to procure our freedom was His own blood. It was the giving of His life that guaranteed our deliverance and lasting freedom from demonic powers that previously held us captive.

Jesus gave Himself as the ransom to set us free from sin. Someone had to enter Satan's slave market, and Jesus chose to be the one. Someone had to offer the price, and Jesus offered to pay the price for our freedom with His own blood. Someone had to finalize the deal, so Jesus willingly paid the price with His own life on the Cross.

The truth is, many people would buy a slave from the slave market, use them for a while, and then put them back on the trading block to sell them again. Jesus didn't do that. When He bought us, He delivered us from the sickening state of slavery forever! He *permanently set us free* from Satan's control and the power of sin — this is what the word *exagoradzo* means.

How Should We Respond to All This?

Because we were bought with the highest price — the precious blood of Jesus — Paul said, "…Therefore glorify God in your body, and in your spirit, which are God's" (1 Corinthians 6:20). As a child of God, you've been translated out of the kingdom of darkness and into the kingdom of God's dear Son (*see* Colossians 1:13). You are not your own; you belong to Jesus.

Remember, "Christ hath redeemed us from the curse of the law, being made a curse for us…" (Galatians 3:13). Therefore, darkness and all the effects of darkness are to no longer be part of your life. Things like sickness, poverty, fear, and strife are all part of darkness and therefore have no place in you. God's will is for you to receive His healing in your body, to be blessed with prosperity in your finances, and to experience His supernatural peace in your mind and emotions.

In our next lesson, we will turn our attention to the third Greek word used to describe "redemption," the word *lutroo*, which means *to set a captive free by the payment of a ransom.*

STUDY QUESTIONS

Study to shew thyself approved unto God, a workman that needeth not to be ashamed, rightly dividing the word of truth.
— 2 Timothy 2:15

1. It's extremely important to realize that your salvation had *nothing* to do with you and *everything* to do with God. According to Paul's words in Romans 3:10-12 (Psalm 14:2,3), what was your condition *before* coming to Christ? What did Jesus say in John 6:44 and 65 was the only way you could be saved?

2. In this lesson, we learned that before we repented of our sins and asked Jesus to be our Lord and Savior, we were *spiritually dead* and *demonically energized* by Satan (*see* Ephesians 2:1-3). Thank God He didn't leave us in that deplorable condition! What does Paul identify in Ephesians 2:4-9 as God's motive for saving you? And *how* are you saved?

PRACTICAL APPLICATION

> But be ye doers of the word, and not hearers only,
> deceiving your own selves.
> — James 1:22

1. Can you remember what your life was like before you heard the Gospel and accepted God's free gift of eternal life through Jesus Christ? How would you describe the *pre-salvation* you?

2. What Jesus accomplished through His death and resurrection is absolutely extraordinary! How have these lessons helped you better understand and appreciate what He has done for you? How have they changed your opinion of yourself as a treasured child of God?

3. Why not take some time right now to praise God for all He's done. As only you can, tell Him how much you love Him and thank Him for all the many ways He has transformed and blessed your life. He is worthy of your worship and loves to hear it from your lips!

---

[3] Rick Renner, *Dressed To Kill* (Tulsa, OK: Harrison House, 1991, paperback edition 2015), pp. 94,95.

[4] Rick Renner, *Sparkling Gems From the Greek, Volume 1* (Tulsa, OK: Harrison House, 2003) p. 63.

TOPIC

Paying the Demanded Price

SCRIPTURES

1. **Psalm 107:2** — Let the redeemed of the Lord say so, whom he hath redeemed from the hand of the enemy.
2. **1 Peter 1:18,19** — Forasmuch as ye know that ye were not redeemed with corruptible things, as silver and gold...but with the precious blood of Christ....
3. **Titus 2:14** — Who gave himself for us, that he might redeem us from all iniquity, and purify unto himself a peculiar people, zealous of good works.

GREEK WORDS

1. "redeemed" — λυτρόω (*lutroo*): a price paid to purchase a slave from the slave market, thus making the newly purchased slave the buyer's personal property
2. "redeem" — λυτρόω (*lutroo*): a price paid to purchase a slave from the slave market, thus making the newly purchased slave the buyer's personal property

SYNOPSIS

During the First Century, when the apostle Paul had an extended time of ministry in the city of Ephesus, he was given a firsthand view of one of the largest slave markets in the entire Roman Empire. People came from all over the region to buy and sell slaves. It was during Paul's stay in Ephesus that he developed the concept of *redemption*, which he based on the slave market.

In Greek, the word for a *marketplace* is *agora*, and it is from this word that the word *agoradzo* was developed. It means *I buy* or *I redeem*, and it was particularly known as the word for *a slave market*. Oftentimes, the prefix *ex* was connected in front, forming the word *exagoradzo*, which means *to buy out of*. This word depicts the buying and selling of slaves and particularly portrays one who comes into the market and buys a slave *out of* that horrible place to permanently set him free. That is where the word "redemption" comes from.

When Jesus came into the world, the world was a slave market very similar to the markets that sold slaves like the one in the lower part of the city of Ephesus. When man fell in the Garden of Eden, all of humanity became enslaved in Satan's slave market. Moved by His indescribable love and compassion, Jesus chose to come to earth and give His life to purchase us out of Satan's power and dominion and set us free forever. Willingly, He paid the demanded price for our *permanent* liberation.

The emphasis of this lesson:

Another Greek word used to describe our redemption is the word *lutroo*, and it means to set a captive free by the payment of a ransom. This word informs us that our freedom was not really free but *extremely expensive*. The ransom Jesus paid to secure our freedom was His own blood.

Uncommon Facts About Slaves That May Surprise You

For most of us, when we hear the word "slave," a certain image comes to mind. We usually think of people dressed in ragged clothes doing hard, menial labor. We imagine common laborers like brick layers, road builders, construction workers, or farm hands. But in the ancient world, that was not always the case.

Although it may seem unthinkable, there were quite a number of slaves that were highly skilled. In fact, many were very educated and their gifts and talents highly valued. Those who belonged to wealthy masters often held trusted positions as household or palace stewards, financial managers, or secretaries. Some slaves were famous philosophers, school teachers, store managers, and even doctors. Thus, slavery was not just for low-level, poorly-educated people. It also included highly-skilled, highly-educated, well-dressed individuals that would be considered the upper echelon of society.

Although some slaves were assigned menial tasks that Romans considered too low for them to do themselves, other slaves were given vital tasks like educating the children of rich Roman families. Physically, slaves looked so much like the rest of the population, the Roman senate once considered mandating that slaves wear special clothes to identify them as slaves.

What's also interesting is how much the value of slaves varied. One could be purchased for as little as 500 denarius or as much as 875,000 denarius, depending on their physical condition and skills. For example, a simple slave girl could be bought for as low as 1,800 denarius, where as a more beautiful slave girl could cost as much as 6,000 denarius.

Male slaves with a good physique, special skills, and higher education could cost an enormous sum, and Romans preferred male slaves because men were physically able to do more tasks than women. By law, slaves were not permitted to own anything — not even the clothes they wore. And if a master eventually freed his slave, it gave the former slave a great measure of freedom and liberty.

What Is the Significance of These Facts?

Oddly enough, what's true about slavery in the physical realm is also true about slavery in the spiritual realm. It doesn't matter who you are or what kind of clothes you wear or what neighborhood you grew up in. You can be a Wall Street executive, a renowned architect, a college professor, or a billionaire businessman, but if your life has not been touched by the grace of God, you're in spiritual slavery.

The fact is, everyone born into this world, regardless of status or financial affluence, is born into sin and bound in Satan's slave market. They may look very professional, be highly educated, wear the finest clothes, and live in the most expensive homes in the world. But until they surrender their life to Jesus and His blood cleanses their spirit, soul, and body, they are still a slave in Satan's slave market.

The Bible clearly states that before we are saved, we are all "the servants of sin" (see Romans 6:17, 20). The word "servants" here is taken from the Greek word *doulos*, which is a term for the most wretched slave in the New Testament. It depicts *one totally sold into slavery* or *a perpetual slave for life*. It denotes *one bound to do the bidding of his owner, a slave whose principal task was to fulfill the desires of his master for the rest of his life*. It is a picture of one whose will is completely swallowed up in the will of another.

By using the word *doulos* — translated here as "servants" — Paul tells us that before we were saved, we were "swallowed up" in the will of Satan. Although we may have thought that we were in charge of our lives and the ones calling the shots, in reality, we were miserable slaves to sin and our futures were being coordinated by an unseen, diabolical spirit that wanted to destroy us.

But then Jesus Christ saw us and was immediately moved with compassion to set us free from Satan's slave market. "Whatever the price is," Jesus said, "I will pay it to make them mine." The Bible says Jesus "...made himself of no reputation, and took upon him the form of a servant, and was made in the likeness of men: and being found in fashion as a man, he humbled himself, and became obedient unto death, even the death of the cross" (Philippians 2:7,8).

Friend, Jesus died so that you could truly live. He paid the ultimate price to *redeem* you and make you a joint heir with Him. You are no longer a slave to sin but a servant of righteousness.

We Have Redemption Through the Blood of Jesus

The third Greek word used to describe "redemption" in the New Testament is taken from the word *lutroo*, which describes *a price paid to purchase a slave from the slave market, thus making the newly purchased slave the buyer's personal property*. It means *to set a captive free by the payment of a ransom*, which is exactly what Jesus Christ did for each of us.

In order for a buyer to obtain the slave of his choice, an extremely high price had to be paid. If he greatly desired a certain slave, the auctioneer could demand an unreasonably high price. The use of this word *lutroo* to denote the redemptive work of Christ on our behalf informs us that our freedom was not really free. On the contrary, our freedom was *extremely costly*.

In fact, the price Jesus paid for us was the highest price ever paid for a slave in the history of mankind. What was the ransom Christ paid to secure our freedom from Satan's ownership? He purchased us with His own blood. This fact is noted again and again throughout Scripture:

- **Ephesians 1:7** says, "In whom we have redemption *through his blood....*"

- **Colossians 1:14** says, "In whom we have redemption *through his blood*...."
- **Colossians 1:20** says, "And, having made peace *through the blood* of his cross...."
- **Hebrews 9:12** says, "...But *by his own blood* he entered in once into the holy place, having obtained eternal redemption for us."
- **1 Peter 1:18,19** says, "Forasmuch as ye know that ye were not redeemed with corruptible things, as silver and gold...but with the *precious blood of Christ*...."

It was the shedding of Jesus' own blood that guaranteed our deliverance and lasting freedom from demonic powers that previously held us captive. This word *lutroo* — which describes our redemption — unmistakably means that Jesus paid the ransom that set us free! *He bought us with His own Blood.*

Then when we come to Titus 2:14, the Bible declares that Jesus gave *Himself* as the ransom in order to set us free. It says, "Who gave himself for us, that he might *redeem* us from all iniquity, and purify unto himself a peculiar people, zealous of good works." The word "redeem" in this verse is taken from the Greek word *lutroo*.

This means that the word *lutroo* in Titus 2:14 conveys this idea:

[Jesus] who gave Himself for us, that He might purchase us out of the slave market to become His own personal property — yes, He was willing to pay the ransom price to see us liberated and set free....

A price had to be paid, and Jesus paid it with His own life and His own blood on the Cross. In our final lesson, we will look at the fourth word used in the New Testament to describe our *redemption*, the word *apolutrosis*, which helps let us know that Jesus restored us to full status.

STUDY QUESTIONS

Study to shew thyself approved unto God, a workman that needeth
not to be ashamed, rightly dividing the word of truth.
— 2 Timothy 2:15

1. When you hear the word "slave," what image comes to your mind?

2. Out of all the "uncommon facts" about slaves, what surprised you most? Why?

3. The ransom Jesus paid to secure our freedom from Satan's ownership was His own blood. History records that the blood of Jesus Christ was poured out at the whipping post where He was scourged and at the Cross where He died. How powerful is Jesus blood? Look up these verses and identify what Jesus' blood provides for you:

   • Matthew 26:27,28

   • Romans 5:9

   • Colossians 1:20

   • Hebrews 9:11-14

   • Hebrews 10:19,20

   • 1 Peter 1:18,19

   • 1 John 1:7

   • Revelation 1:5

PRACTICAL APPLICATION

**But be ye doers of the word, and not hearers only,
deceiving your own selves.
— James 1:22**

1. After hearing about all that Jesus did to redeem you — including the great sacrifice of His own body and blood — what are you most grateful for?

2. In what practical ways can you repay Jesus for what He did for you?

3. Are there any areas in your life where you have backslidden into some kind of bondage that once held you hostage? If so, what are they?

4. Take some time to close your eyes and quietly reflect on the high price Jesus paid to purchase your freedom and rescue you from Satan's control and the power of sin. Repent of anything that may be keeping you from intimacy with Him and tell Him how much you love Him.

TOPIC
Restored to Full Status

SCRIPTURES

1. **Psalm 107:2** — Let the redeemed of the Lord say so, whom he hath redeemed from the hand of the enemy.
2. **Ephesians 1:7** — In whom we have redemption through his blood, the forgiveness of sins, according to the riches of his grace.
3. **Romans 3:24** — Being justified freely by his grace through the redemption that is in Christ Jesus.
4. **1 Corinthians 1:30** — But of him are ye in Christ Jesus, who of God is made unto us wisdom, and righteousness, and sanctification, and redemption.
5. **Colossians 1:14** — In whom we have redemption through his blood, even the forgiveness of sins.

GREEK WORDS

1. "redemption" — ἀπολύτρωσις (*apolutrosis*): from ἀπό (*apo*) and λυτρόω (*lutroo*); the word ἀπό (*apo*) means back, and λυτρόω (*lutroo*) means to pay a ransom for a slave's permanent freedom; compounded, to pay the price required to buy back a slave with the intention to give him freedom
2. "bought" — ἀγοράζω (*agoradzo*): to purchase in the marketplace; used to denote the purchase of a slave out of the slave market; to transfer ownership from a seller to a buyer; to redeem
3. "redeemed" — ἐξαγοράζω (*exagoradzo*): a compound of the words ἐκ (*ek*) and ἀγοράζω (*agoradzo*); ἐκ (*ek*) means out and ἀγοράζω (*agoradzo*) means to purchase in the marketplace; used to denote the purchase of a slave out of the slave market; to transfer ownership from a seller to a buyer; to redeem; when compounded into ἐξαγοράζω (*exagoradzo*), it pictures one who has come to purchase a slave OUT OF the slave market

4. "redeemed" — λυτρόω (*lutroo*): a price paid to purchase a slave from the slave market, thus making the newly purchased slave the buyer's personal property

SYNOPSIS

In 1882, Fanny Crosby wrote one of the most memorable hymns of all time titled "Redeemed, How I Love to Proclaim It." It has been sung by countless Christians from all walks of life for nearly 140 years, and its message is just as real and just as powerful today as the day it was written. The first verse says:

> Redeemed, how I love to proclaim it!
>
> Redeemed by the blood of the Lamb;
>
> Redeemed through His infinite mercy,
>
> His child and forever I am.

And the chorus says:

> Redeemed, redeemed,
>
> Redeemed by the blood of the Lamb;
>
> Redeemed, redeemed,
>
> His child and forever I am.

If you have been saved by Jesus Christ — washed by His precious blood and forgiven of your sins — you are *redeemed*! And it's a big deal! It's no wonder the psalmist said, "Let the redeemed of the Lord say so, whom he hath redeemed from the hand of the enemy" (Psalm 107:2). We were once in the death-grip of the devil, but Jesus came to earth to set us free. By paying the extraordinary price of His life's blood to deliver us from Satan's power, He gave us great reason to rejoice in our redemption.

The emphasis of this lesson:

When Jesus shed His blood and died on the Cross, He paid the ransom for our permanent freedom from Satan's slave market. At the same time, His death and resurrection also restored us to rightstanding with God — reinstating our full status as His sons and daughters. All this mean-

ing is found in the Greek word *apolutrosis*, the fourth word for "redemption" used widely in the New Testament.

As a born-again child of God, you have been set free from Satan's slave market. Jesus paid the price to deliver you from the devil's dominion and the power of sin. You are no longer oppressed and harassed by the detrimental effects of darkness. You are redeemed!

Thus far, we have examined three words used in the New Testament to describe our redemption. They are:

- The Greek word *agoradzo*, which describes *Satan's slave market.*
- The Greek word *exagoradzo*, which means *to be purchased out of that slave market.*
- The Greek word *lutroo*, which describes *the exceedingly high price that was paid for our freedom.*

To Be 'Redeemed' Means Fully Restored to One's Original Condition

The fourth word for "redemption" used widely in Scripture is the word *apolutrosis*. It is a compound of the word *apo*, which means *back*, as in something that is being *returned back*; and the word *lutroo*, which means *to pay a ransom for a slave's permanent freedom.* When these two words are compounded, the new word *apolutrosis* means *to pay the price required to buy back a slave with the intention to give him his full freedom.*

Rick shares further insights on the meaning of this word *apolutrosis* in his book *Dressed To Kill:*

> "This fourth word for 'redemption' tells us God's ultimate purpose in redeeming us from Satan's slave market. The word *apolutrosis* ('redemption') most assuredly means that Jesus paid the ransom in order to *return* us to the condition we were in before our captivity began. In the plainest of language, this means that Jesus paid the price to permanently set us free and to *restore* us to the full status of sons [and daughters of God]!
>
> Paul uses the word *apolutrosis* in this very way in Ephesians 1:7 when he says, 'In whom [Christ] we have *redemption* through his blood, the forgiveness of sins, according to the riches of his grace.'

By choosing to use the word *apolutrosis* ('redemption'), Paul declares that we were forever delivered from Satan's power — we were forever removed from that dreadful place — and now we have been *fully restored* by the blood of Jesus Christ and *placed back into a state of rightstanding with God.* We are fully restored and fully set free from Satan's former grip over us!

This is why Galatians 4:7 declares, 'Wherefore thou art no more a servant, but a son; and if a son, then an heir of God through Christ. Romans 8:17 proclaims that we are so entirely restored through the blood of Jesus that we have now become 'joint heirs' with Jesus Christ Himself!"[5]

So in addition to Jesus buying you back and setting you free from Satan's dominion, His redemption also includes the idea of *full restoration* back to the original plan God had for you from the foundation of the world. God designed for you to be a free, full-fledged son or daughter of His. This freedom and intimate relationship with the Father was lost when Adam and Eve rebelled against God's word. In that moment, sin and death entered the world, and all of humanity from that point on was born into Satan's slave market. But when Jesus came and paid the price to ransom us, He transferred our ownership from Satan's custody to Himself, and He also restored us to the original status as God's sons and daughters.

Your Reinstated Status As God's Son or Daughter Is Declared Again and Again

There are a number of examples of this word *apolutrosis* used in the New Testament. In addition to its use in Ephesians 1:7, the apostle Paul also uses it in several other verses, such as Romans 3:24, which says we are, "…justified freely by his grace through the redemption that is in Christ Jesus." Again, this word indicates we were not just purchased out of slavery, but also fully restored to our original condition.

The word *apolutrosis* is also used in First Corinthians 1:30, which says, "But of him are ye in Christ Jesus, who of God is made unto us wisdom, and righteousness, and sanctification, and redemption." The word "redemption" here is the Greek word *apolutrosis*, which includes the idea of being restored to the original status as God's sons and daughters.

The apostle Paul also used the word *apolutrosis* in Colossians 1:14 when he declared, "In whom we have redemption through his blood, even the forgiveness of sins." Once more, we see the Greek word *apolutrosis* — here translated as "redemption" — and in this case, the Bible says that the redemptive work of Jesus Christ has provided us with the *forgiveness of our sins*. Hence, we're not trying to earn God's forgiveness and rightstanding with Him — we already have it through Jesus' blood.

A SUMMARY OF WHAT IT MEANS TO BE 'REDEEMED'

You Were Once Captive in Satan's Slave Market

Before the grace of God touched your life, you were in bondage that was so complete the apostle Paul said you were "...sold under sin" (Romans 7:14). That word "sold" is taken from the Greek word *piprasko*, which describes *a product for purchase* and literally depicts *a transfer of property*. In this particular verse, it pictures *a slave being transferred into the ownership of a new master*. By using this word, Paul was telling us that mankind had been transferred from God's hands into the hands of a new owner — Satan. And before Jesus came into our lives, Satan had full ownership of us.

What's more, Paul also said that before our salvation experience we were "the servants of sin" (*see* Romans 6:17,20). This word "servants" is taken from the Greek word *doulos*, which is the most abject term for a *slave* in the New Testament. It pictures *one totally sold into slavery — one bound to do the bidding of his owner*. This servant's existence was to service his master in whatever way the master asked or demanded. One expositor has explained that this word *doulos* — translated here as "servants" — describes one whose will is completely swallowed up in the will of another.

Thus, the use of this word *doulos* means that before we were saved, we were "swallowed up" in the will of Satan. Although we may have thought that we were in charge of our lives and that we were calling the shots, in reality, we were miserable slaves to sin, and our destinies were being orchestrated by an unseen, diabolical spirit that wanted to destroy us.

Our pre-salvation slavery to the devil was so deep-seated that our nature became intrinsically interwoven with the seed of rebellion, which is at the very core of Satan's nature. Rebellion against God ran so deep in our blood and became so ingrained in our character that eventually the gulf between

God and us became so great that the Bible says we became "alienated and enemies" in our minds through wicked works (*see* Colossians 1:21).

Your Life Was Dominated and Controlled by Satan

This pervading demonic presence in our lives and in the world around us was absolute and supreme. Paul describes our condition in Ephesians 2:2 saying, "Wherein in time past ye walked according to the course of this world, according to the prince of the power of the air, the spirit that now worketh in the children of disobedience."

Notice the phrase "according to." It is a translation of the Greek word *kata*, which describes *a downward force* that is *dominating* or *controlling*. By choosing this word *kata*, Paul is telling us that before we came to Christ, our lives were not just *influenced* by "the course of this world." They were *dominated, controlled,* and even *manipulated* by it. The phrase "the course of this world" in Greek refers to the popular thinking of a person's own particular time and generation.

So who or what is controlling and manipulating "the course of this world?" Paul said society is dominated by "…the prince of the power of the air, the spirit that now worketh in the children of disobedience" (Ephesians 2:2). Satan is "the prince of the power of the air." Ultimately, he is the controlling force that is manipulating and dominating the unsaved people in society and the world system, which includes governments, entertainment, education, and the court system.

Before we were saved, our entire life was dominated by the enemy who was working through the fleeting whims of society. We were dead in our sins and had no idea of eternal things. As slaves in Satan's slave market, we were slapped around and brutally abused, being sold from one form of bondage into another. Having control over our mind and emotions, the devil did everything he could to take us down and destroy us. We were "servants of sin," swallowed up in Satan's will and dominated by sin's power.

Then Jesus Came To 'Redeem' You and All Mankind

When you — and the rest of humanity — were in the deplorable condition of captivity in Satan's slave market with no hope of release, Jesus came just in the nick of time to "redeem" you. The word **agoradzo** is the first Greek word for "redemption" we learned about, and it means *to purchase* *a slave in the marketplace.* Specifically, this word tells us that Jesus Christ came to earth to *locate us* in our depravity and personally inspect our slavery to Satan.

The second word for "redemption" we examined is the Greek word *exagoradzo.* It is a compound of the word *ek*, meaning *out*, and the word *agoradzo*, which we just saw means *to purchase in the marketplace* and was used to denote *the purchase of a slave*; it carries the idea of transferring ownership from a seller to a buyer. When these two words are compounded to form *exagoradzo*, it pictures *one who has come to purchase a slave OUT OF the slave market.*

The third word for "redemption" that we examined is the Greek word *lutroo*, which describes *a price paid to purchase a slave from the slave market, thus making the newly purchased slave the buyer's personal property.* This word *lutroo* lets us know that Jesus was so dedicated to delivering us from Satan's dominion He was willing to pay the ransom price of His own blood in order to set us free. This was the highest price ever paid for a slave.

In this lesson, we have added one more word for "redemption" — the Greek word *apolutrosis.* It is from the word *apo*, which means *back*, and the word *lutroo*, which we just saw means *to pay a ransom for a slave's permanent freedom.* When these words are compounded to form the word *apolutrosis*, it means *to pay the price required to buy back a slave with the intention to give him freedom.* The use of this word *apolutrosis* tells us that not only did Jesus' shed blood permanently set us free from Satan's slave market, it also met the requirements to fully restore us to our position as sons and daughters of God.

You Are Forever Set Free From Satan's Control

Friend, through the redemptive work of Jesus Christ, Satan has lost all legal rights to you. The moment you put your faith in Jesus and surrendered your life to His lordship, your ownership was transferred out of the devil's hands and into Jesus' hands. The devil no longer has any authority over you, your family, your finances, your business, your body, your mind, your future, or anything else.

Colossians 1:13 and 14 says, "[Christ] who hath delivered us from the power of darkness, and hath translated us into the kingdom of his dear Son: in whom we have redemption through his blood, even the forgiveness of sins."

If you're redeemed, God wants you to open your mouth and declare it unashamedly (*see* Psalm 107:2). In fact, he wants you to boldly share the truth about Jesus' redemptive work with those who are lost and still a part of Satan's slave market. Jesus paid a high price for them to walk in freedom — He gave the ransom of His own life and blood. That is what redemption is all about!

STUDY QUESTIONS

Study to shew thyself approved unto God, a workman that needeth not to be ashamed, rightly dividing the word of truth.
— 2 Timothy 2:15

1. Can you remember singing songs in church as a child? Did you ever sing the song "Redeemed, How I Love to Proclaim It"? What worship songs do you most remember singing as a child? Which one (ones) were most meaningful to you? Why?

2. When Jesus redeemed you, He paid the price to permanently set you free from Satan's ownership and to *restore* you to the full status of a son and daughter of God. To help you grasp this vital truth, take time to reflect on these passages that declare your position as God's child. What notable character qualities should you demonstrate as a child of God?

    *   John 1:12,13

    *   Romans 8:14-16

    *   2 Corinthians 6:14-18

    *   Galatians 4:4-7

    *   Philippians 2:14,15

    *   1 John 3:1-3

3. Romans 8:17 declares that as fully restored children of God, we are "joint–heirs with Christ." The apostle Paul talks about this in Galatians 3:26-29 and in Ephesians 2:6,7. What do you think it means to be a joint-heir with Jesus Christ?

PRACTICAL APPLICATION

But be ye doers of the word, and not hearers only, deceiving your own selves.
— James 1:22

1. As you come to the conclusion of this study, how has your understanding of your redemption through Jesus Christ been expanded by these five lessons? What are your greatest takeaways from what you learned that you want to remember and share with others?

2. Who do you know and care about that is lost and still a part of Satan's slave market? Begin to pray diligently for God to remove the blinders from their eyes, soften their hearts with His love, and give them the measure of faith to believe and receive Jesus as their Lord and Savior.

---

[5] Rick Renner, *Dressed To Kill* (Tulsa, OK: Harrison House, 1991, paperback edition 2015), pp. 98.

Notes

Notes

Notes

Notes

_____

_____

_____

_____

_____

_____

_____

_____

_____

_____

_____

_____

_____

_____

_____

_____

_____

_____

_____

_____

_____

_____

_____

_____

_____

_____

_____

Notes

www.ingramcontent.com/pod-product-compliance
Lightning Source LLC
Chambersburg PA
CBHW071747020426
42331CB00008B/2214